Splish·Splash Science

Learning About Water With Easy and Fun-Filled Activities!

By Rebecca Olien

SCHOLASTIC
PROFESSIONAL BOOKS

NEW YORK • TORONTO • LONDON • AUCKLAND • SYDNEY
MEXICO CITY • NEW DELHI • HONG KONG

For my husband, Joel

Interior design by Kathy Massaro
Interior illustrations by James Graham Hale
ISBN: 0-590-11595-2
Copyright © 1998 by Rebecca Olien
All rights reserved.
Printed in the U.S.A.

Contents

Introduction

Water fills our oceans, rivers, puddles, pipes, and bodies. We depend on it, yet often take it for granted. Children love to splash, sip, and swim in it, but as teachers we can help them discover more: the properties of water and important ways water can be used and protected. The activities in this book use an exploratory approach that encourages children to investigate, question, and discover the hows and whys of water.

Water is one of the most available materials teachers have on hand: almost every classroom is equipped with a sink. We can pump it, pour it, mix it, or drip it. We can absorb it, freeze it, melt it, condense it, boil it, evaporate or vaporize it, even dissolve substances in it. Water affects everything it comes in contact with. It gives life to plants and animals, causes rocks to weather and change form, dissolves minerals, rusts metal, puts out fires, and pushes up on whatever is on or in it. There are so many stories to tell about water, so many discoveries to make about what it does, that this book can only open the eyes of students and, hopefully, make them curious to find out more.

The following chapters offer you many different opportunities: from helping children observe the tiny world of a water drop to exploring the much larger waters of a pond and the creatures that live there. You'll also find critical thinking questions to help students explore further. Each student will prepare a Science Journal, a special place where he or she can jot down questions, record observations, illustrate and explain thoughts and ideas. The Journal also provides a visual account of student learning.

Many of the activities in this book integrate science with other subject areas. I have found that making connections between the disciplines helps children learn and retain more. Literature Connections offer fiction and nonfiction books to be read aloud or made available for children's self-selection.

I have attempted to vary the activities to provide students with different learning settings. Besides whole-group instruction, you'll find opportunities for partner projects, independent learning, and small group studies. Discovery Stations—centers where children can pursue learning on their own—pose questions and opportunities to challenge them further.

In his work as a plant physiologist, my father searches for ways to develop plants that can withstand the cold of winter. At an early age I looked at his magnified photographs of ice crystals inside plant cells. The crystals were beautiful. How could they be so damaging to the life of the cell? I learned from my father's work that simple things such as water are not always so simple. There is still much to be learned. I hope these activities give you and your students similar gifts from the world of water.

—Rebecca Olien

CHAPTER 1

Getting Started

What do your students already know about water, and what do they want to learn? What are some ways they can record their ideas and find out more? Use the following ideas and activities to begin your exploration of this topic.

Science Journals

Science is the perfect subject to motivate young children to practice writing. I have found that, with a little encouragement, children are eager to share questions and observations about a given topic, especially one where they can use their senses to explore. To give them a place to record these elements of learning, have each student make a Science Journal. Here students are free to explain, question, predict, and tell about what they know and what they wonder about. With a bit of modeling and a few prompts, even young children are able to record their learning in a meaningful and useful way.

What Does a Science Journal Look Like?

Students can use an ordinary spiral or loose-leaf notebook as a Science Journal or make a simple one for themselves. A 12- by 18-inch piece of tagboard, folded in half and decorated, makes a sturdy cover. Punch holes along the folded edge and attach punched papers to the inside of the cover with brass fasteners or yarn. You may also want to add the Science Journal pages included with the activities presented here. These can be glued into children's spiral or loose-leaf notebooks, or added as pages in the self-made Journals.

The content of a Science Journal might include a collection of writings, drawings, activity sheets, charts, lists, and cut-out pictures. Each child's Journal reflects his or her own style as the unit progresses, since each child is at a different ability level. Beginning writers may need to rely more heavily on invented spelling; or they may find it easier to express their thoughts through drawings. You can always add captions or labels to clarify when needed.

From time to time, you may want to choose from the Critical Thinking Questions included to suggest starters for Journal entries; or you may use

students' open-ended questions. Using children's own questions encourages them to expand their higher-level thinking. Try providing free writing time after a stimulating activity or a particularly good class discussion. Children may express themselves in ways different from what you intended, providing you with opportunities to find out what captured their attention.

When you are ready to begin, choose one or more of the following warm-up exercises.

Opening Prior Knowledge Questions

Help students "get their feet wet" about this topic by responding to the following questions in writing, or with pictures on large easel paper. When you have completed the unit, revisit the same questions as part of your evaluation process. Explore any new information students can add.

1. What different ways do we use water?
2. What special properties or characteristics does water have?
3. Where does water come from?
4. How is water important to people?
5. What else do you know about water?

Learning Webs

Help children prepare a water "learning web" for their Science Journals. Begin by writing the word *water* inside a big circle on the chalkboard. Have students do the same in their Journals. Now, make a web of ideas that connect to the topic of water. Before writing, help students brainstorm ideas. You might need to add a couple words yourself to get them started. Be sure to include water attributes as well as water uses. If you prefer, prepare one large learning web that can stay up in the classroom throughout the unit. Students can add new words and categories as they acquire new concepts.

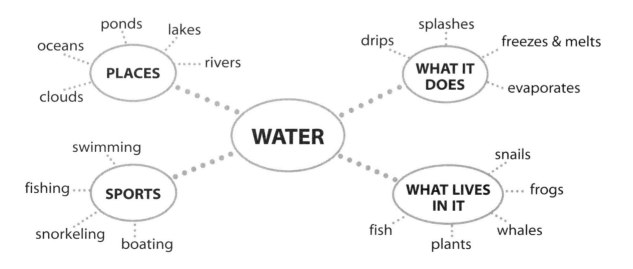

Water Pictures

Have children cut out water-related pictures from magazines and newspapers. They can paste the pictures into their Journals and label with captions. Encourage them to write about what is happening in the picture and why water is important. Ask: How is the water being used? What is the water doing?

KWL Chart

Make a large KWL (Know—Want to know—Learned) wall chart. As a class, fill in the first two columns. Keep this chart on the wall during the unit so that children can add or revise information as they discover more. Students can also add copies of the initial chart to their Science Journals in order to enter their own ideas to the "Learned" column. I have found this a useful evaluation tool for students to keep track of what they are learning.

Water Word Wall

Use journal page 9 to get students thinking about water words. (*splash, trickle, waves, sparkle, shore, flood, puddle*) Have them write their favorites in the drops. To help students spell words correctly, fill in larger paper drops with words children tell you. Place these on a Water Word Wall. Students can add new words of their own as the unit progresses. Referring to these words will also help students as they write in their Journals.

Name _____

Water Words

9

Make a Splash!

Now it's time for you to jump into your unit and "make a splash!" Indoors and out, the activities in this chapter will help your students look at and think about water in new ways.

A Cup of Water

What could be simpler than studying a cup of water? It might sound easy, but this activity sharpens observation skills and gets students thinking about some water-related concepts that often lead to further questions and exploration.

Materials

clear plastic cups • water • plastic spoons • colored comic strips • journal page 11

What to Do

1 Give each student a cup of water. Have students look carefully at their cups of water and write down everything they notice. The large cup on the journal page works well as a recording sheet, since students can easily draw and label what they see, such as a drop running down the side of the cup.

2 Encourage students to look closer by asking questions: Do you see air bubbles in the water? Is there water on the outside of your glass? Children notice other things that aren't always expected. Have them share their discoveries with the class and record these in their Science Journals.

3 Hand out the spoons. Ask: How can the spoon change the way the water looks? (By stirring, it can make waves, ripples, drips, etc.) How does the water change the way the spoon looks? (It makes the spoon look larger, bent.) Have students hold their spoons behind their cups and look through the cups at the spoons. Ask: How does the spoon look now? What other observations can you make?

4 Hand out the comic strips. Ask: How does the cartoon look when you put it behind your cup of water? Now set your cup of water on top of the cartoon. What do you notice? (The water enlarges or magnifies the art.) Give students time to share and record what they observed.

Teacher TIP

Aerate the water before filling the cups by shaking the water in a jar to mix in some air. You can also refrigerate the water, or use ice water, to promote condensation on the outside of the cups.

Name _____

Exploring Water in a Cup

11

Water Charades

Put a new spin on the familiar game of charades: Invite students to pantomime different ways that water is used. And keep this game in mind if you're planning a wrap-up celebration at the end of your water unit. Students will enjoy sharing their pantomimes with others.

Materials

activity page 13 • scissors

What to Do

1. Cut apart several sets of water charade slips. Save the blank slips for students to write their own ideas on.

2. Begin by playing with the whole class. Mix the slips in a box or coffee can. Choose a student to draw a slip and act out what is indicated (or a team of students can act out the same thing together).

3. Have the rest of the class try to guess what activity the pantomime shows. Remind them that all the actions include water in some way.

4. The first student (or team of students) to guess correctly will be the next to choose a slip.

5. Challenge students (or teams) to come up with new water uses to add to the blank slips.

Teacher TIP

Students might not understand some of the actions, such as those indicating scuba diving or surfing. Display pictures that show people engaged in different water sports. You may also display objects from different water activities, such as fishing lures without hooks, a snorkel tube and goggles, flippers, and so on.

Water Charades

go fishing	run through a sprinkler
swim	brush teeth
dive	go canoeing
go surfing	give a cat a bowl of water
wash clothes	wash dishes
wash the car	feed the fish
put out a fire	drive a motorboat
drink at a water fountain	go down a water slide
water the garden	take a bath
wash a dog	
scuba dive	
water ski	
walk in the rain	

Pick a Puddle

Puddles are wonderful "mini" water environments. They are fun to explore after a rain, or you can make your own.

Materials

puddles (or buckets of water) • chalk • string • scissors • tape measure • yardsticks • journal page 16

What to Do

1 Divide the class into small groups. Locate a puddle for each group or make puddles by dumping out buckets of water where water will collect. You can ask students to help choose the best puddle places.

2 Have students work in groups to complete the following tasks. They should record their findings on the journal page.

- Use chalk to trace a line around the puddle. Watch to see if the puddle changes shape or size after a time. Ask: Where did the water go? How could we find out? (See Chapter Four, "Disappearing Drops," for more.)

- Ask students to estimate how big around they think their puddle is and wind string around the perimeter. Cut the string and hold it along a tape measure to measure.

- Plunge the yardstick into the deepest part of the puddle to measure the puddle's depth.

- If the puddle has been standing for awhile, look for animal and plant life (including the greenish tinge of algae) in and around the water.

- Ask: What can float in the puddle? (Try a twig, pinecone, leaf, seed pod.) What sinks? (pebble, sand, etc.)

3 Compare data recorded about each group's puddle. Ask: Who had the puddle with the largest perimeter? Who had the deepest puddle? Were all the puddles the same shape? What interesting things did you find out about your puddle?

Critical Thinking Questions

How long do you think the puddles will last? Is the largest puddle always the deepest? Where could we pour water to make the deepest puddle? What effects might a puddle have on the plants and animals that live nearby?

Extensions

- If you created your own puddles, have students try this activity again after a rain and compare how the natural puddles are the same or different from the ones they made.

- Watch different puddles change over time. Ask: What makes some change faster than others? (amount of sunlight, weather conditions, ground slope, etc.)

- Ask: Have you seen large puddles that stay wet all spring? What lives in these puddles? What makes these puddles go dry?

- Write stories about being tiny and going on a journey across the puddle. Help students brainstorm ways they could cross the puddle and what adventures they might have. This can be a story written together as a class, or everyone can write their own and combine their stories into a class book.

- After a particularly rainy day, have students become puddle engineers. Design ways to connect as many puddles as possible. Later, draw maps to show their waterways and float toy boats on them. (See Chapter Seven, "Boat Making," for more.)

Literature Connection

- *Puddles*, by Jonathan London, makes a good introduction to the puddle activity and gets kids in the mood for exploring.

- Read Chapter Six of *The House At Pooh Corner* by A.A. Milne. Play a version of Pooh Sticks on a windy day. Students choose a twig and place it on the puddle's edge. The student whose twig reaches the other side first, wins.

- For a funny story about a pig who does not want to leave her muddy puddle, read *The Piggy in the Puddle* by Charlotte Pomerantz. Children will love to hear the rhyming, tongue-twisting words over and over.

Name _____

Pick a Puddle

1 Draw the shape of your puddle here. Draw it again after some time. How did it change shape?

2 What is the perimeter of your puddle? (How big around is it?)

My estimate _____   How it measured: _____

3 How deep is your puddle? _____

4 Do you see anything alive in or near your puddle? Draw pictures here:

5 What floats in your puddle? _____

_____

What sinks? _____

_____

Splish-Splash Science   Scholastic Professional Books

CHAPTER 3

Diving In

Submerge students further into the world of water by transforming your classroom. This chapter presents ideas for creating a stimulating interactive environment—one that evokes curiosity and challenges children to become actively engaged.

Water Wall Bulletin Board

Cover a large bulletin board with blue paper. This is your Water Wall. Use child-drawn pictures to create a watery habitat such as a pond or wetland. (For resource materials, see "Classroom Resources," Chapter Eight.) Have students paint pictures of different animals that live in the water. For students who need ideas, place names of animals in an envelope and have them choose one. Don't forget to include the names of insects, birds, amphibians, and reptiles, besides different kinds of fish and mammals.

Once the paintings dry, invite students to add details with markers. Then have them cut out their animals and attach them to the Water Wall. Add pictures of logs, plants, rocks, or whatever else is needed to give the animals their intended habitat. Students may continue to add pictures as the unit progresses or use the wall as a Discovery Station.

You can also use the Water Wall to play a game of "I Spy." In this game, the students take turns asking questions about an animal on the wall which one child spies. Children take turns asking questions such as What color is it? How big is it? Does it have fins? The first child to guess the correct animal is the next spy.

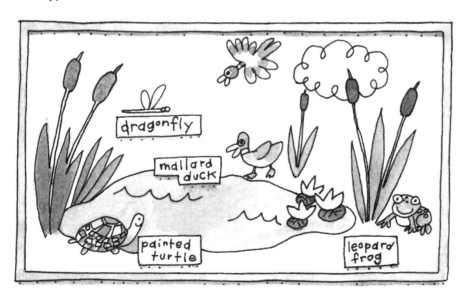

Teacher TIP

The Water Wall can also be used for many language arts and research lessons. Have students either research and write labels providing information about each of the animals or connect animals together with yarn to show food webs. Students might ask questions about the animals, locate and display books to help research the answers, and make their own books that describe what they found out.

Poetry Poster: "Water"

Display the poetry poster (bound in the back of the book) on a bulletin board. Read the poem aloud and ask children to search for words and phrases the poet uses to describe the many forms water takes. Then invite students to offer their own impressions of the different "sounds and moods and colors" of water by writing their own poems. Refer them to the Water Word Wall for ideas. (See page 8.) Students might also like to draw or bring in pictures of the different states of water described in the poem and write captions for their pictures to mount alongside.

Water View

Windows are a perfect place to add a display. Cut out transparent blue plastic (the type used for overheads or report covers) in the shape of water drops. Dampen one side of each drop and stick it to the window. Ask: How long do you think the water will hold the drops to the window? Have students record guesses and actual results in their Science Journals. Children will see how water can work like glue (adhesion), as well as view the world through water drops.

Discovery Stations

Set up and use discovery stations in your classroom to challenge children to explore a topic further. They are designed so that children can use the materials without adult help and make discoveries for themselves. They also provide opportunities for you to meet some of the diverse needs of your students. Some stations are self-explanatory; others require simple directions that can be written on a card, recorded as a message on a tape player, or demonstrated once to the whole class.

Since most stations are designed for individuals or small groups of two or three students, you can set up a Discovery Station around a low table, counter, upside-down milk crate, or portable plastic tub. This makes it easy to move, rotate, or change the station as interest, time, and space dictate. Students can go to the stations as part of free-choice time, when they have finished their work, as a reward, or as part of a rotating science lesson.

The following Discovery Stations can be set up at any time during the unit; they also work well as unit openers. Start out small with one or two stations, then add more as the unit progresses. For additional ideas, use some of the Extension Activities that appear throughout this book.

Water Table

Set up an area with a water table, a wading pool, or a large plastic tub along with water-conveying implements such as turkey basters, plastic eyedroppers, funnels, plastic tubing, pumps taken from cleaning bottles, empty liquid-soap bottles, and various other different-sized containers. Place your container on top of a plastic tarp. Then fill it with water. To begin, encourage children to experiment freely by manipulating the equipment. Other ideas for using the water table for more structured investigations may develop as the unit progresses. This is a place, for example, where students can float their ice cubes (Chapter Five) or test their boats (Chapter Seven).

Magnetic Water Words

Set up a writing station where students can have fun placing magnetic words together in different combinations to create water sentences and poems. To make the magnetic words, write water words (taken from the Water Word activity in Chapter One) and several copies of other connecting words (*on, in, it, the, is,* etc.) on small pieces of tagboard. Place a piece of adhesive magnetic tape on the back of each word. Provide a magnetic chalkboard, or use a metal cookie sheet (not aluminum), to hold the students' creative placement of the words. Put the words in a basket and challenge children to arrange them into sentences or poems about water. Have them copy their favorite writing into their Science Journals.

Laminate some blank pieces of tagboard and fasten magnetic strips to the backs. Children can use an overhead pen to write extra words on the laminated strips. After they are done, the laminated surfaces can be wiped with a damp towel, ready for the next student to use.

Water Writing

This is a different type of writing station that works well for the younger, kinesthetic learner. Provide students with small containers of water, different items to dip, and various surfaces to write on. For example, cotton swabs can be dipped in water and used on small slates, fingers can be used to dip and write on cork board, or small paintbrushes can be dipped and used on the classroom chalkboard. Have students practice writing their water words. Besides helping them learn vocabulary and spelling in a tactile way, they will also notice the effects of water on different surfaces.

Listening Station

Set up a tape recorder with headphones at this station for students to listen to water sounds. An audiotape can be purchased at a science supply store, or made by recording your own water sounds. For example, you might record the sound of a faucet dripping, a bath shower, rain, a sprinkler, a gurgling brook, or ocean waves. Provide paper and crayons for children to draw pictures of what they think of as they listen to the sounds. If you make your own recording, record a number before each new sound on the tape. Students can write the corresponding number on a paper and write their guess for the water source of each sound. When you are ready to put the station away, play the recording for the class and reveal where each water sound was recorded.

Creative Dramatics

Provide a collection of water-related puppets and plush animal toys with which students can create stories. (Try to keep the animals from the same water habitat so that children don't form misconceptions about what animals live together. For example, if you include a seal with a beaver and an otter, children might become confused about a seal's habitat.) Use a curtain in a doorway, a large refrigerator box, or a table turned on its side for a puppet theater. Note that it is easier for some children to manipulate a stuffed animal than a puppet.

Art Station

Watercolors Let children use heavy watercolor paper and watercolor paints to experiment with mixing colors with water. Tell children to use a crayon to draw simple shapes. Using small paintbrushes, have them paint clear water in these shapes. Next, while the paper is still wet, have students dab different colors in the water and watch the water mix and flow with colors. Set aside to dry.

Collage Ask children to cut water-related pictures from magazines and glue them on cardboard to make a collage. Help children notice the many different colors and textures of water.

Straw-Blower Art
Use white construction paper, water colored with tempera or food color, small paintbrushes and straws. Students dip the brushes and drip drops on their paper. They use the straws to blow the drops around the paper and make designs. Set aside to dry.

Food Color Tie-Dye
Use paper dinner napkins and several cups of different, diluted food colors. (Four or five drops of color in each cup of water works fine.) Fold and roll the napkins into interesting shapes and dip portions into different colors, giving the colors time to bleed and run together. Carefully open up the napkins and set aside to dry.

CHAPTER 4

Explorations in a Drop

Use these easy-to-do experiments to help students explore science concepts such as cohesion, surface tension, and evaporation.

Do Drop

With just one drop of water, children can observe how it moves, how it keeps its shape, and how it is attracted to other drops to form larger drops.

Teacher TIP

Let students have fun with an eyedropper and a cup of water before you attempt to use eyedroppers in an activity. This way children won't feel pressure using one for the first time. For those who have trouble, fill the dropper for them and let them practice squeezing out the drops. Later, show them how to squeeze and release the bulb in the water to fill it. Most children learn to do this quickly if given time to "play." If some still have trouble, let them make drops by rolling water from their finger or the tip of a spoon, or by working with a partner who can help.

Materials

waxed paper • 4- by 6-inch pieces of cardboard • tape • eyedroppers • toothpicks • plastic cups • water • newspaper • book • Science Journals

What to Do

1 Cut waxed paper into pieces slightly larger than the cardboard. Attach the waxed paper to the cardboard pieces by folding over the edges and taping it to the back.

2 Cover desks with newspaper. Give students waxed paper cards, cups of water, eyedroppers, and toothpicks.

3 Tell students to place a water drop on the cards. Ask them to observe its shape and draw a picture of what they see in their Science Journals. Encourage them to look at the drop at eye level. Ask: How does it look? (rounded)

4 Have students poke the drops with their toothpicks. Ask: What happens? (The drop stays the same rounded shape.) Can you split your drops into two drops? (Yes, but it's hard to do. The drop wants to stay together.) Have them record what happens in their Science Journals.

5 Instruct students to put more drops onto the card. Tell them to roll the drops around with a toothpick. Ask: What happens when the drops touch? (They jump together to form one drop.)

6 Show students how to support one end of the cardboard with a book. Then give them the opportunity to have water-drop races with a friend by placing drops at the top of two cardboard pieces at the same time.

Critical Thinking Questions

Do other liquids form drops the same as water? How could we find out? (Try oil, rubbing alcohol, hydrogen peroxide.) Have students record their experiments in their Science Journals.

Extension

DROP RACES Here's another kind of race children enjoy: Sprinkle six drops of water on a 8- by 12-inch piece of waxed paper. Blowing through a straw, children see how fast they can push the drops together to form one big drop.

Literature Connection

After observing the properties of water, students will be fascinated by Walter Wick's *A Drop of Water*. Spectacular close-up photos show water in its various states—as droplets falling and splashing, steam, snowflakes, and ice.

Science Background

A water drop holds its shape remarkably well on waxed paper, even when you poke it with a toothpick and pull it around. What makes the "skin" that holds it together? Actually, two forces are at play: cohesion and surface tension.

Inside the drop, the water molecules are strongly attracted to each other and repelled by the wax in the paper. The attractive force between the water molecules is called cohesion. When you bring two water drops close enough on the waxed paper, they jump together because of this internal, cohesive effect.

Cohesion also causes the molecules at the surface of the drop to be pulled inward. There is no opposing pull from the air or the waxed paper. This creates surface tension, which acts like a skin to hold the drop together, even when you move it around.

Penny Drops

Students observe cohesion and surface tension at work when they heap water on a penny, drop by drop.

Materials

paper towels • pennies • cups • water • eyedroppers • journal page 25

What to Do

1 Ask students to estimate how many drops of water they can pile on a penny before they spill off. Have them record their estimates on their journal page.

2 Give each student a penny placed on a paper towel so that they can more easily see the water when it spills off.

3 Have students count the number of drops they can pile on the penny, slowly adding one drop at a time, and then record the number on the reproducible.

4 Repeat the experiment two more times. Ask: How much do your numbers change? What do you think might cause you to get different numbers?

5 Ask students to observe and record on the reproducible the water dome that forms. Explain that water has something like a "skin" that helps it stick together and form the rounded shape. We call this skin *surface tension*.

Critical Thinking Questions

Would oil heap on a penny as well as water? How could you find out? Have students record their investigations in their Science Journals.

Discovery Station

Stock a center with several nickels along with eyedroppers and a cup of water. Ask: Knowing how many drops fit on a penny, how many drops do you estimate will fit on a nickel? Try it and see!

Name _____

Penny Drops

How many drops of water can you pile onto a penny?

	My Estimate	**My Results**
Test 1		
Test 2		
Test 3		

Look at the pile of water on the penny. Look at it from the side.
Then, draw how it looks.

Break Down

In this easy-to-do activity, students quickly see how soap breaks the surface tension of water.

Materials

waxed paper • water • cups • eyedroppers • liquid soap • toothpicks • Science Journals

What to Do

1 Hand out waxed paper, water in cups, eyedroppers, and toothpicks. Have students drip several drops of water on the waxed paper and poke the drops with toothpicks. (The drops hold together.) They should use pictures and words in their Science Journals to record what happens.

2 Give each student a drop of liquid soap. Instruct them to dip their toothpicks into the soap and poke their water drops. Ask: Now what happens to the drops? (The water drop loses its shape when it is touched by the soap.) Use pictures and words to record what happens.

Discovery Station

Make a sign that asks, "How many drops of soapy water can you pile on a penny?" Provide cups of soapy water, eyedroppers, paper towels, and pennies with which students can investigate.

Science Background

When you touch soap to a drop of water, what makes the drop lose its rounded shape? Before you touched the drop with soap, the surface tension between the water molecules held the drop together in a heap. But add soap molecules and you break the surface tension. This is because the soap molecules have a water-loving end that grabs onto the water molecules, and breaks the tension between them. For a fun demonstration, put water in a pie pan and sprinkle pepper evenly over the top. Dip a toothpick into detergent and touch it to the water's surface in the middle of the pan. What happens? As the soap molecules break the surface tension, the pepper flies to the edges!

Disappearing Drops

*C*hildren explore evaporation as they measure the time it takes for a drop of water to "disappear."

Materials

eyedroppers • cups • water • clock or watch • Science Journals

What to Do

1 Ask children what they know about evaporation. Where have they experienced water evaporating? (clothes drying on a clothesline; puddles disappearing; sweat drying off their skin) If necessary, provide a few examples.

2 Let children estimate how long they think it might take for one drop of water to evaporate. Ask: How could we find out? Help students design an experiment that keeps track of one drop of water until it evaporates. Questions to consider: On what kind of surface should the drop be placed? Where in the room should the drop be placed? How should we time it as it evaporates? Students may do experiments individually or as a class, taking turns watching. Have them record their experiment and results in their Science Journals.

Critical Thinking Questions

After the activity, ask students to make true statements about their results. For example, "The drop on the windowsill disappeared first." Then ask, How might we change where we put the drop to make it evaporate faster? Slower?

Discovery Station

Using a clear cup of water, have students predict and then test how long it will take for all of the water to evaporate. Draw a line with a marker on the outside of the cup to show the level of water each day. Invite students to apply what they learned from "Disappearing Drops" to this activity. Where should they place the cup?

Science Background

*W*hat causes water to evaporate? When you place a drop of water on a sunny windowsill, for example, the molecules in the drop heat up and move faster and farther apart. This allows the water molecules to escape into the air. When this happens, the water molecules are no longer visible because water is changing from a liquid to a gas, called water vapor. In addition to heat, evaporation rates may vary due to humidity and air currents.

Super Soaker or Water Proofer?

Children make predictions about and observe how water is absorbed or repelled by different surfaces. To report, they organize their findings on a large wall chart.

Materials

food coloring (any color) • water • plastic cups • eyedroppers • newspaper • a collection of scraps of different types of paper (construction, tissue, paper towel, newsprint, notebook, shelf liner, wax, heavy brown paper bag, crepe paper, gift wrap) • hand lenses

What to Do

1 Make a wall chart on large paper. Title it "Super Soaker or Water Proofer?" Draw lines to divide the chart into three sections. Label the first section "Super Soaker," the second "O.K. Soaker," and the third "Water Proofer."

2 Mix food coloring in small cups of water so that it makes a bright color.

3 Ask: Which of these different scraps would you use to dry your hands after washing them? We'll call those "Super Soakers." Have students select the scraps and place them on a flat newspaper-covered surface.

4 Ask: Which would you use to cover up in a rainstorm? We'll call those "Water Proofers." Have students select the scraps and place them on a separate newspaper-covered surface.

5 Using the eyedroppers, have children put one drop of colored water on each sample to see how it is absorbed. (They may want to watch with hand lenses.)

6 Ask: Which samples soaked up the water fastest (or left the largest spots)? Which kept the water from soaking in? Have students revise their predictions and glue the results on the classroom chart, choosing the best section for each sample.

Extension

SPLISH-SPLASH COLLAGES Invite students to glue the Soakers and Proofers, as described in the previous activity, into a textured collage that separates the two kinds. Have them use eyedroppers to splash the collage with brightly colored water. When dry, title the collages and make a display that shows the two different results.

Drops in a Bucket

Students will love estimating how many drops of water there are in a bucket. Even more, they'll love finding out. Use this simple lesson in math to show how to solve big problems with several smaller solutions.

Materials

eyedroppers • teaspoon and cup measures • bucket (any size) • water • calculators • Science Journals

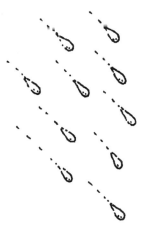

What to Do

1 Fill a bucket with water and challenge students to estimate how many drops of water they think there are in the bucket. Have them record their estimates in their Science Journals.

2 Invite children to think of ways to find out how many drops there are. Review their ideas, discussing the practicality of each.

3 Then tell them that there is a trick mathematicians use when determining very large numbers. The trick is to first find out how many drops there are in much smaller volumes, then multiply.

4 Have students count and record the number of drops of water there are in a teaspoon. Then have them measure and record the number of teaspoons of water there are in a cup.

5 To show the number of drops there are in a cup, use calculators to multiply the number of drops in a teaspoon by the number of teaspoons in a cup. For younger students, you may want to draw the actual number of teaspoons and drops inside. This will help them visualize that the new number represents what you would get if you added up all the drops in the teaspoons.

6 Now have students count and record the number of cups of water it takes to fill the bucket.

7 To find the number of drops in the bucket, multiply the number of drops in a cup (step 5) by the number of cups in the bucket. Again, use pictures to help younger students visualize.

Critical Thinking Questions

How do your final numbers compare with your estimates? How do they compare with the final numbers recorded by other students? Why might these numbers be different? (The size of the drops may vary, as will the amount of water in the teaspoon and cup measures.)

Discovery Station

Some students may want to count the number of drops to see how close their number comes to the number they arrived at through multiplication. Set this up as an extended activity or as part of a discovery station. Either way, share the results and invite other methods for checking the answer.

Stir It Up

Water, when you add it to something, often causes some kind of change to happen. In this activity, children observe ways common substances react with water.

Materials *(for each group)*

6 spoons • 6 clear plastic cups of water • plastic egg cartons • sugar • salt • sand • cornstarch • flour • cooking oil • journal page 32

What to Do

1 Cut egg cartons in half so that each group has six connected cups. Place one or two teaspoons of sugar, salt, sand, cornstarch, flour, and cooking oil in separate compartments of the egg carton.

2 Have students work in groups. First, have them predict what will happen when they stir a spoonful of each substance into a cup of water. Then, have them add the substance and stir to try to make the substance dissolve (disappear) and record what happens on the journal page.

3 Have children summarize their observations and write these on the chalkboard. Ask: Which substances were you able to make dissolve? Which settled to the bottom? Which stayed suspended in the water? Which floated on top?

4 Challenge students to come up with ways to try to make the undissolved substances dissolve. After these trials, explain that some substances are "water-loving" and readily dissolve, while others, such as oil and flour, are "water-hating" and will never dissolve.

Extension

Students may think that the sugar and salt literally disappear when they dissolve. To help them understand that these substances are still in the water, try this: Fill a clear plastic cup with water and mark the water level on the cup before and after adding salt or sugar, a teaspoon at a time. Then have students observe the difference.

Name _____

Stir It Up!

What happens when you mix each substance with water? Put a ✓ in the chart to show your results.

Substance	Dissolves	Settles to the Bottom	Stays Suspended	Floats on Top
Sugar				
Salt				
Sand				
Cornstarch				
Flour				
Oil				

Splish-Splash Science   Scholastic Professional Books

CHAPTER 5

States of Water

One of the wonderful things about studying water is the ease with which it can be used to study the three states of matter. The transformation of water from a solid to a liquid to a vapor or gas can be easily explored in the classroom.

Ice Cube Close-up

Let children take a close-up look at an ice cube and draw inferences about water in its solid state.

Materials

clear plastic cups • water • ice cubes • Science Journals

What to Do

1 Pass out cups half-filled with water. Ask students to predict if an ice cube will float or sink in the water. Have them give reasons for their predictions. If necessary, direct them to think about experiences where they have seen ice either sink or float. Have them record their predictions in their Science Journals.

2 Pass out the ice cubes and have students place one in their cup of water. Have them record their observations in their Journals next to their predictions. Ask: Does the whole ice cube float on top of the water, or just some of it? Be sure to draw your cube showing how much is above water and how much below.

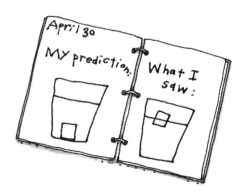

Science Background

As water cools, it becomes denser until just above the freezing point. Then, as it cools to freezing, ice crystals begin to form and the volume expands, making the ice less dense than liquid water. This is unusual, as most liquids contract and are denser in their solid state.

Why does ice float in water? An ice cube floats because it displaces (or pushes out of the way) a volume of water whose weight is equal to its own. Although children should not be asked to understand these concepts, they will be able to make interesting observations about the way water behaves in its solid state.

33

Critical Thinking Questions

How is water in its solid form different from water in its liquid form? (It's cold and hard when you touch it; it stays separate from the water; it's lighter than water.) If the ice cube were bigger, would it sink? How could we find out? (Using the same amount of water, add a bigger ice cube.)

Extension

Ask children: Do other liquids float when frozen, or is water special? How could we find out? Try freezing other liquid substances, such as cooking oil or rubbing alcohol, and placing the frozen substance in the same substance in liquid form. Ask: How are they like water? How are they different?

Literature Connection

Add a poetic dimension to your ice studies with *Once Upon Ice and Other Frozen Poems*, selected by Jane Yolen. Children will enjoy "frozen" poems about icicles, ice cubes, and more by noted poets X.J. Kennedy, Mary Ann Hoberman, Lee Bennett Hopkins and others. Gorgeous color photographs of ice in natural settings complete this wonderful collection.

I'm Melting!

In this activity, students work in cooperative groups and hold a contest to see which team can melt an ice cube most quickly.

Materials

ice cubes • aluminum pie pans • student-inspired materials • paper and pencils

What to Do

1. Explain to students that their challenge is to see which group can melt an ice cube most quickly. Have students brainstorm, in groups of three or four, all the ways they can think of to melt an ice cube.

2. Next, have them circle the ideas that could work in the classroom and give them time to collect the materials that they will need.

3. The following day, pass out the ice cubes, and pie pans to catch the melt, and watch the fun. After the contest is over, discuss which techniques worked the best. Ask: Why would breaking ice into smaller pieces make it melt faster?

Extension

Instead of trying to melt an ice cube, hold a contest to see which group can keep ice frozen the longest when stored at room temperature.

Literature Connection

After students conduct their investigations into melting, check your library for *Emily's Snowball: The World's Biggest* by Elizabeth Keown. Students will enjoy tracking the progress of Emily's snowball that grows bigger and bigger—until the warm spring weather arrives.

Science Background

What melts ice fastest? Pouring hot water on ice is one of the fastest ways because heat comes into direct contact with the ice. Another effective method is crushing ice. By increasing the ice's surface area, it comes into contact with more warm air. Salting the ice also works well. When salt is sprinkled on a piece of ice, some of it dissolves in the small amount of liquid on the ice's surface. This salt solution has a lower freezing point than pure water. (That's why using salt on icy roads will help to melt ice and keep it from refreezing.)

To keep an ice cube from melting, materials with air pockets help reduce the transmission of heat. Cotton balls, crumpled waxed paper and sponges work well because the air spaces in these materials create an air pocket between warm air in the room and the ice. The same principle is at work in fiberglass insulation and Styrofoam picnic coolers.

Freeze It

What happens to water when it freezes? Children design an experiment to find out.

Materials

student-inspired materials to conduct the test • water • Science Journals

What to Do

1 Ask: Does water shrink or grow when it freezes? How could we find out? Help students design an experiment and test their ideas. (They might mark the water level on a plastic cup, for example, and freeze the water to see if the ice is above or below the line.)

2 Ask: Did the water grow or shrink when it turned to ice? Have students record the experiment in their Science Journals.

Critical Thinking Question

What do you think would happen if we filled a plastic container with water, sealed the lid on tight, and put it in the freezer? (The lid of the container would pop off under the pressure of the expanding ice.)

Extension

RAINBOW ICICLES If you live in a cold climate, try making icicles in the winter. Poke a pinhole in the bottom of a plastic gallon jug. Hang the jug outside, if possible, by your classroom window. Watch the water slowly drip and freeze into an icicle. Add more water as needed to keep the jug from freezing or as water runs out. Try adding food coloring to create rainbow icicles.

Literature Connection

Enhance your ice explorations with the book *Very Last First Time* by Jan Andrews. In northern Canada, along the seacoast, an amazing phenomenon occurs in the winter. When the tide goes out, the thick ice stays intact and forms a ceiling over the dry seabed. In this story, a young Inuit girl ventures out over the seabed to collect mussels before the tide rushes back in.

Cloud Makers

Making investigations about how clouds are formed helps students understand the water cycle.

Materials

a humidifier • clear plastic cups • ice cubes • hot tap water • Science Journals

What to Do

1 Show students the humidifier. Let them see you add the water, turn it on, and watch the cloud that forms. Ask them to compare the humidifier cloud with a cloud in the sky.

2 Review the concept of evaporation as explored in Chapter Four. Explain how water from oceans and lakes evaporates into water vapor. It then forms clouds of tiny water droplets similar to the one forming in the room.

3 Pass out two clear plastic cups to each student. Explain that they are going to make their own little "cloud" inside the cups. Show them how one cup can be turned upside down to cover the other cup.

4 Pour about a half inch of hot tap water into one of the cups at each student's desk. Have them quickly turn their other cup upside down over the first.

5 Allow students to observe and record in their Science Journals what happens inside the cups. Ask: Where do the water droplets come from?

6 Now explain that they are going to try to make rain. Since cold air can't hold as much water as warm air, you will put ice on the top cup to cool the air inside the cups.

7 Pass out ice cubes to place on the top cup. Have students record in their Journals what they see. (Water droplets form on the underside of the top cup and drip into the water below.)

Water-Go-Round Wheel

Students combine science and art to make a 3-D water cycle wheel that shows water's journey.

Materials

activity pages 39 – 40 • thin cardboard or old file folders • brass fasteners • scissors • glue • cotton balls • yellow and blue cellophane • glitter • black markers • crayons

What to Do

1. Pass out copies of the activity pages for each student to glue onto a piece of cardboard. Then have students cut out the two wheels along the dotted lines.

2. Invite students to cover the sun, ocean, and river on the wheel with small pieces of yellow and blue cellophane.

3. Give students small pinches of glitter to glue onto the arrow going to the cloud. Explain that we can't see water vapor, so the glitter shows the path the water vapor takes.

4. Let them pull apart cotton balls and glue thin pieces onto the clouds on the wheel. Ask: What happens to the water in the cloud? Have children show rain by placing tiny drops of glue on their wheel along the arrow running from the cloud to the lake. For a rain cloud, students may darken the cloud in this frame with a black marker.

5. Ask: Where else does the rain go? Have children color the river blue and the land green and brown.

6. Have students use a brass fastener to connect the wheels, placing the one with pictures behind the other. The top wheel should move around freely. To see the phases of the water cycle, students turn the wheel.

Literature Connection

- *The Stream* by Naomi Russell features engaging foldout pages that follow the birth of a stream through its journey in the water cycle.

- For a rich sensory experience, use *Rain*, a wordless picture book by Peter Spire, to encourage children to use water words to describe what is happening on each page.

Going in Cycles

Use the Going in Cycles read-aloud play on pages 41 and 42 for students to act out a short play about the water cycle. Let children take turns performing the different parts in groups of six. Afterward, ask students to explain what is silly and what is true about this play. (Water drops don't talk, and are not perfectly shaped; water changes when it evaporates from a liquid to a gas; etc.)

Setting: Hang a big paper cloud from the ceiling with string. Paint a 2- by 6-foot piece of cardboard blue and scallop it at the top to look like waves. Prop this upright on the floor between stacks of books. Hang white and blue crepe-paper streamers from the cloud to the waves.

Costumes (optional): Make blue tagboard water drops with circles cut at the top for faces.

Name _____

Water-Go-Round Wheel

(TOP WHEEL)

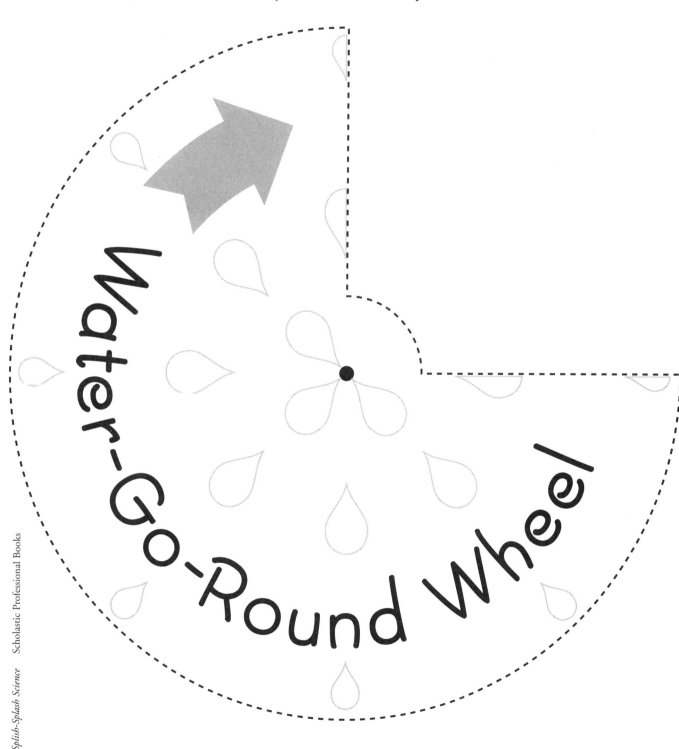

Water-Go-Round Wheel

Name _____

Water-Go-Round Wheel
(BOTTOM WHEEL)

Splish-Splash Science Scholastic Professional Books

Going in Cycles

Characters
Water Drops 1, 2, 3, 4, 5, and 6

(Drops 1, 2, and 3 are behind the waves. Drop 1 is bouncing up and down playing, while Drops 2 and 3 are swaying back and forth.)

Drop 2:   Hey, Drop! Take it easy.

Drop 3:   Yeah, you're making a splash.

Drop 1:   Don't be drips. Have some fun!

(Drop 4 enters, jumping loudly as it joins the other drops.)

Drop 4:   Yee ha!! What a ride!

Drop 2:   (to Drop 4) Where did you come from?

Drop 4:   The same place you did.

Drop 3:   What do you mean?

Drop 4:   (pointing up to the cloud) From a cloud, of course.

(Drop 5 enters the same way as Drop 4.)

Drop 5:   Wowee! Just thought I'd drop in.

(Meanwhile, Drop 1 looks up at the streamers, gently holds them, then twirls around and goes offstage.)

Drop 2:   And I suppose you came from the cloud, too?

Drop 5:   Yes. It was a most amazing thing. One minute I was feeling light and bouncy. Then I grew cold and turned into a water blob like you. I fell right through the cloud.

Drop 3:   I'm not a blob. I'm a perfectly shaped drop.

Drop 2:   Hey, where did the other drop go?

(Drop 6 enters with a jump. Drop 2 looks up and exits as Drop 1 did.)

Drop 6:   Yippee! That was fun. Next time, I want to come down as hail.

Drop 3:   Hey! Something funny is going on here. You drops keep coming. But I'm sure there were some other drops here a minute ago-o-o-o!

(Drop 3 twirls offstage.)

Drop 6:   Feel free to vaporize. I'm going to go with the flow for awhile.

(Drop 6 relaxes by closing eyes and swaying back and forth. Opens eyes as Drops 1, 2, and 3 return, plopping into the water.)

Drops 1, 2, and 3:   You were right. We did come from the clouds.

Drop 4:   That's okay. You didn't remember. We all get a little dizzy from going around in cycles.

Drop 5:   Now that we're all together, let's make a wave.

(Drops all move up and down to make a wave as at a football game, then wave good-bye.)

The End

Cloud Watching

Invite children to identify cloud types and learn about weather patterns they suggest.

Materials

journal pages 44–45

What to Do

1. Ask: Do clouds always look the same? What colors can clouds be? Have you ever been in or above a cloud? Discuss.

2. Pass out copies of the Kinds of Clouds Chart. Explain that scientists group clouds and give them different names. Read about the types of clouds described on the chart. Ask: Are there clouds in the sky today? If so, what kind of cloud on the chart do they most look like? From looking at the sky, do you think it will rain soon?

3. Pass out the Cloud Watching Charts. Have students fill in the cloud type and cover in the first column on the chart under Day 1. Keep track of the sky for five days, having students describe and record the type of clouds and cloud cover they observe each day.

Critical Thinking Questions

Have you ever seen more than one cloud type in the sky at the same time? What do you think this event might say about the coming weather? (It's changing.)

Extension

Let students use cotton balls, blue construction paper, different combinations of white and black paint, and paper plates to make different cloud types. Then have them write the cloud names on their paper-plate sky.

Literature Connection

Children will enjoy Armstrong's adventure as he takes a trip on a cloud in *Cloud Nine* by Norman Silver. After reading this story, discuss what is true and false about clouds in the book.

Safety Note

When students are watching clouds, warn them against looking directly at the sun.

Science Background

The chart on page 45 includes basic cloud types that are easy to recognize and signal weather conditions fairly consistently. Keep in mind, however, that no cloud-watching experience is complete without noting wind speed and direction, the presence of warm and cold fronts, temperature, barometric pressure, humidity, and how clouds change over time.

Name _____

Cloud Watching Chart

Draw these symbols on your chart to show how much clouds cover the sky each day.
Then use your Kinds of Clouds Chart to record the number of the kind of cloud you see.

◯ Clear   ◖ Partly Cloudy   ● All Cloudy

	Day 1	Day 2	Day 3	Day 4	Day 5
Cloud Cover					
Kind of Clouds					

Kinds of Clouds Chart

③ Cumulus

Big, puffy clouds that can look like animal shapes.
These are fair-weather clouds, but can change into cumulonimbus clouds.

⑤ Stratus

Low layers of clouds that make a drizzly day.
They cover the sky in a thick blanket of gray.

② Cirrocumulus

These clouds are high in the sky.
They form a pattern like fish scales.
They tell that a change in the weather is coming.

① Cirrus

Wispy, high clouds, sometimes called horses' tails.
These clouds mean that a change in the weather is coming.

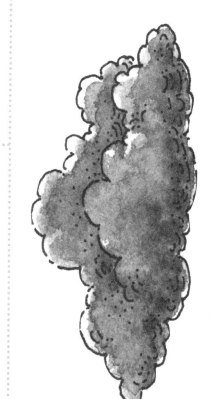

④ Cumulonimbus

These towering thunderheads are sometimes called King of the Clouds.

CHAPTER 6

Water Life

So far, students have looked at water as a substance, exploring its different properties and uses. In this chapter, they focus on ways water is important to life on our planet.

Something Fishy

Goldfish are common pets, but children know surprisingly little about them. In this activity, students make and record observations about how goldfish are adapted to a watery life.

Materials *(for each group)*

clear plastic or glass quart-size container • goldfish • elodea plant
(for each student) journal page 48

What to Do

1 Obtain the fish and plants from a pet store. The day before you plan to do this activity, fill containers with tap water and let stand for 24 hours.

2 Introduce fish and plants into the containers.

3 Split the class into groups and have them brainstorm and record questions they have about goldfish. Have students draw from memory in their Science Journals what a goldfish looks like and make notes about how it survives in water.

4 Hold a discussion to answer some of the questions. Those that can't be answered easily should be recorded for further exploration. Have books about goldfish on hand for research.

5 Give each group a fish to observe. Draw a large outline of a goldfish on the chalkboard. Have student volunteers add different parts of the fish (eyes, fins, gills, mouth) on this outline. Label the parts.

6 Hand out a copy of the journal page and have students observe their fish, draw a picture of it, label any parts they can identify, and answer the following questions.

- Look at your fish's eyes. How are they adapted for seeing underwater?
- Look at your fish's mouth. What happens when it opens underwater?
- Look at the fins. How do they help the fish live underwater?
- Find the fish's gills. The gills help the fish breathe by taking oxygen out of the water. What do you have that helps you breathe instead of gills?
- Can your fish hear if you make a noise? Can it see you? How could you find out?

Critical Thinking Questions

Ask students to look at the drawing of a goldfish which they made from memory. How is it different from the drawing made from observation? What are some important ways a goldfish is adapted for life underwater? Ask: If you had to live underwater, what adaptations would you need?

Literature Connection

Children will enjoy making their own fish pictures after reading *The Rainbow Fish* by Marcus Pfister. They can decorate them with glitter to make them sparkle as in the book.

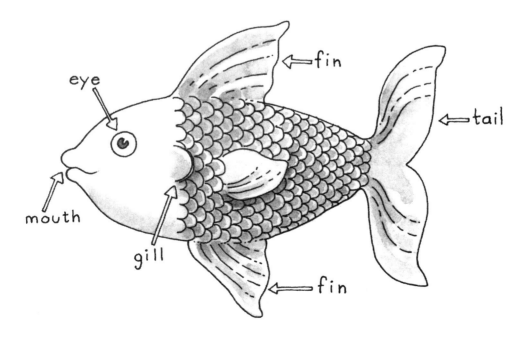

Name _____

Something Fishy

Draw a picture of your fish.
Label any parts you see.

Splish-Splash Science   Scholastic Professional Books

The Classroom Pond

If you find it too difficult or expensive for students to visit a water environment, here's how you can bring one to them. Studying the plants and animals in this classroom pond will generate lots of questions that students can record in their Journals for later research. Do this activity in late spring when aquatic life is active.

Materials

plastic tarp • small wading pool • pond water and bottom muck • plastic jars • aquarium fishnets • strainers • plastic spoons • hand lenses • field guides • journal page 51 • Science Journals

What to Do

1 Set up the pond area by placing the pool on top of the tarp in an area of your classroom where children can crouch around the perimeter. Fill the pool with three or four inches of tap water. Let sit for 24 hours.

2 Collect two or three large buckets of pond water. Be sure to collect bottom muck, sticks, floating plants, and rocks, as these are places where many creatures live.

3 Empty the buckets into the pool and allow the water to settle for a day or so.

4 Give children time to look for water life. Show them how to use plastic spoons to turn over rocks and sticks to find aquatic insect larvae. Explain how many of these larvae will change into flying insects in their adult stage. For closer observation, help children scoop creatures into a plastic jar. Allow the water to settle and use the hand lenses. Have them record their observations in their Science Journals.

5 Use the journal page to have students compare the creatures they find with the pictures. Do any look the same? Use the journal page and other reference books to identify as many of the specimens as possible.

Safety Note

Caution children not to pick up any of the creatures they see, as some pond creatures bite.

Teacher TIP

Laminate several copies of the Freshwater Life journal page so that they won't get ruined if they get wet or muddy.

6 Make a class chart showing the different kinds of creatures found. Use drawings to represent unidentified life forms until they can be located in a field guide.

7 Encourage children to make accurate observations. As they notice something new, have them go back to their Science Journals and add more details to their descriptions. Ask: How does the animal move? Did you see it eat anything? What does it do when it meets another animal? What parts of the animal help it live in the water?

8 Have children look for plant life in the pond. Encourage them to write descriptions and draw pictures of what they see.

9 Keep the classroom pond set up for a week or so, then return the contents to the pond outdoors.

Extension

Depending on your pond source, you can make studies appropriate to your own resources. Possible activities include hatching frog, toad, or fish eggs; studying a turtle and releasing it; and watching snails, mud puppies, or small native fish for a day or so.

Literature Connection

Take a close-up look at dragonflies, turtles, tadpoles, springtails, duckweed, algae and other creatures and plants in a pond ecosystem with *One Small Square: Pond* by Donald M. Silver and Patricia J. Wynne. Lively, informative text; exquisite, detailed illustrations; and simple hands-on activities help bring the world of a pond to life. A comprehensive picture glossary at the end of the book will help students identify the living things they find in their pond samples.

Name _____

Freshwater Life

Springtail

Midge **L**arva

Whirligig **B**eetle

Dragonfly **N**ymph

Backswimmer

Beetle **L**arva

Mosquito **L**arva

Water **B**oatman

Diving **B**eetle

Giant **W**ater **B**ug

Water **S**trider

Snail

(Animals are not their real size.)

Splish-Splash Science   Scholastic Professional Books

Water Habitat Models

Making models helps students understand the different components of a water ecosystem.

Materials

pictures of fresh-water environments (ponds, lakes, streams, wetlands) • aluminum pie pans or disposable bowls • clay • blue plastic wrap or cellophane • crayons • scissors • cardboard • toothpicks • twigs • sand • pebbles • moss • pine needles • dried grasses and flowers (optional)

What to Do

1 Display and discuss pictures of water environments. Ask: What plants do you see? What animals? What does the water look like? What else might live in this environment that can't be seen? Explain that they are going to make models of fresh-water environments as habitats for plants and animals.

2 Pass out the aluminum pans. Have children cover the bottoms of their pans with blue plastic to represent the water. Give students clay to build up the shoreline, leaving an open space in the middle for a lake or a pond, or leaving a band open in the middle for a river. Next, have students landscape their models with twigs, pebbles, and sand.

3 Show students how to make plants. Let them use their imagination! Make pine trees or reeds, for example, by poking pine needles into the clay. Make rushes with colored toothpicks or straw. Bits of brown clay at the tops turn these into cattails. Twigs topped with green paper make bushes or trees. Use green glitter for duckweed or algae in the water. Flatten tiny balls of green clay for lily pads.

4 Draw animals or cut pictures from magazines. Glue these onto cardboard and tape them to toothpicks to poke into the clay. Children also like to form three-dimensional animals from clay. Since you will add water to the models when they are complete, make sure water animals such as frogs or fish are made from plastic clay so they can get wet.

5 Use cups to pour water carefully into the models. Display the models with names for each kind of water environment.

Ask: In real life, what might harm your environment? List possibilities on a chart. Ask: How would you feel if someone dumped garbage into your environment? How would you feel if the plants were pulled out or the animals taken away? Explain how this is like what people sometimes do to a real water environment. Help students create a water environment protection plan and list rules for water use next to their models.

The *One Small Square* series by Donald M. Silver and Patricia J. Wynne provides excellent visuals of different water ecosystems. Look for *Pond*, *Seashore*, and *Swamp*.

Drink Up

U se this activity to help students understand the importance of water for good health.

Materials

water • plastic cups • fruit or vegetable such as apple or celery • quart-size measuring cup

What to Do

1 Have students drink water as you discuss its importance for good health and survival. Ask: How do you know when your body needs a drink of water? What are some times when you get thirsty? (when you eat too much salt or sugar; when you exercise) Explain that people can get sick or even die if they go without water for too long.

2 Explain that plants have roots to take in water from the soil, but we get water from food and drink. Ask children to think of juicy foods that might have a lot of water in them. Give children a fruit or vegetable and have them notice the water as they eat it.

3 Tell children that most people should take in about 2 quarts of water each day. To help children visualize this amount, ask them to measure and pour 2 quarts of water into plastic cups.

Science Background

L and-loving plants and animals are made up mostly of water, and it is vital for them to take in water to grow and reproduce and to replace the water given off as waste. Plants usually take in water through roots in the soil, but people and other animals have to drink it or get it through the different foods they eat.

About 60 percent of your body weight is water. To keep healthy, doctors recommend that you take in about 2 quarts of fluid each day. You can do this by drinking water or other liquids and by eating juicy foods. This replaces the water you lose when you sweat, go to the bathroom, and exhale (water vapor). You also need to take in extra water when you eat too much of some substances, such as salt or sugar. The extra water helps your body flush out these substances.

CHAPTER 7

Water Use

Most of us use water so frequently, we aren't aware of the many different ways that we use it. In this chapter, students discover the variety of roles water plays in their lives and think about ways to conserve it.

Count the Ways

Use this warm-up activity to help students brainstorm ways they use water during the day, at home, and at school.

Materials

Science Journals

What to Do

1 Seat children together in groups of three or four. Hold up a glass of water. Ask: What are some different ways we can use this glass of water?

2 Have the groups brainstorm and record their ideas in their Science Journals. At first, they might think only of drinking it. If so, you can ask: Is there enough water in the glass to brush your teeth? Have them write this idea down. Then give them time to think of other possibilities. (wash hands, rinse a dish, etc.) Compile the groups' ideas into one class list.

3 Ask them to brainstorm and list ways a bathtub filled with water could be used. (take a bath, wash clothes, etc.) Compare this list to the first one.

4 Estimate: How many times a day do you use these different amounts of water? How could you find out?

Literature Connection

Help children explore the many ways we use water with the book *Water* by Frank Asch.

How Much Water Have You Used Today?

Students investigate the answer to this question as they keep a diary of all the ways they use water, at home and in school, in one day.

Materials

Science Journals

What to Do

1 Review: What are some different ways we use water? (Refer to "Count the Ways," page 54.)

2 Explain to children that they are going to keep a diary of all the ways they use water in one day, both at home and in school.

3 Start by having them write down all the ways they used water at home that morning. Then have them record all the ways they use water during the school day. Remind them to write in their Science Journals before they go to bed, listing how and when they used water at home.

4 The next day, have students compare the different ways they used water with the lists they made in the previous activity.

5 Ask them to write a few sentences in their Science Journals explaining how water is important to them.

Critical Thinking Questions

Why is it important not to waste water? Think again about the different ways you used water. How might you have used less?

Science Background

How much water do you use everyday? Here are some rough numbers.

One flush of the toilet: 5 gallons

One bath: 27 gallons

One 10-minute shower: 60 gallons

One washing machine load: 30 gallons

One dishwasher load: 10 gallons

One load of hand-washed dishes: 7 gallons

Water Poem Mobile

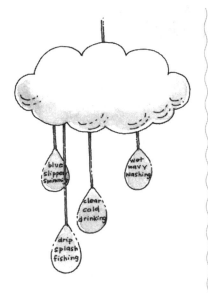

Using ideas and vocabulary gathered from previous activities, students write water poems about how water is used and copy them onto water drops to create a water mobile.

Materials

light-blue paper raindrops • two large paper clouds • blue yarn • colored markers • tape

What to Do

1 Generate a list of water words with the class which describe how water is used. (See "Water Word Wall," page 8, or "Count the Ways," page 54, for ideas.) Write these words on the chalkboard. This is the first list.

2 Ask students for words that describe how water feels, tastes, looks, or sounds. Make a second list.

3 Show children how to select words from each list to make word groups that make sense and sound good together. Do this by choosing a word from the first list and stacking two words from the second list on top of it. For example:

blue
slippery
swimming

drip
splash
fishing

clear
cold
drinking

4 Have children copy their three-word poems onto paper raindrops, writing the last word in a different color so that the water use stands out. Tape the poems to pieces of blue yarn and attach them to a paper cloud. Glue another paper cloud over the first to conceal the taped yarn. Hang the mobile and enjoy a shower of poems!

.... Literature Connection ....

Listen to the Rain by Bill Martin, Jr., and John Archambault is a great book to use as a warm-up for this activity. The authors use poetic and descriptive language to describe a rainstorm, from beginning to end.

Build a Better Boat

By testing their handmade boats, children discover ways to make different kinds of boats float and move on the water.

Materials *(for each group)*

Styrofoam cups and trays • plastic cups • toothpicks • construction paper • aluminum foil • nonhardening clay • straws • plastic container (shoe-box size) • water • a handful of pennies

What to Do

1 Divide the class into groups and give each group the materials listed above. Challenge students to use the materials in different ways to make boats. Ask: Whose boat will carry the most cargo (pennies) without sinking? Increase discovery and creativity by encouraging all attempts.

2 Fill the large plastic containers with water when students are ready to test their boats. Have them keep track of the number of pennies their boats can hold before sinking.

3 Ask questions to help students problem-solve and create better boat designs. For example: How can we change the boat to keep it from tipping? What could we change to keep the boat from sinking?

Extension

Let children make sails for their boats and set them in a bigger pool. Have races by blowing on the boats with straws or by flapping pieces of cardboard. Afterward, challenge children: Can they design a balloon-powered boat?

Literature Connection

Sail Away, by Donald Crews, gives children a view of sailing and teaches a few sailing words along the way. Your students will enjoy reading along in this colorful book.

Science Background

When you put a boat in water, the water pushes up on the boat. Water pushes up on anything you put on or in it. But when the downward push from the boat's weight is greater than the upward push of water, the boat sinks. For a boat to float, water has to push up enough to overcome the downward push of the boat.

How can you change a boat to keep it from sinking? You have to decrease its downward push on the water. You might change its shape to make it flatter or add some air-filled object. That way, you will decrease the downward push of the boat so the water can keep it afloat.

Sudsy Surprise

Children know that they are supposed to use soap to get something clean, but does soap really make a difference?

Science Background

How does soap help water clean? To find out, first experiment with water and oil. Pour a teaspoon of salad oil into a small jar of water. What happens? The oil stays separate from the water, no matter how you shake it. That's because oil molecules, the tiny building blocks that make up oil, are water-hating. The oil pushes away from water, making it hard for water to grab onto it and wash it away.

When you add soap, however, something new happens. Soap molecules have one end that loves oil (or oily dirt) and grabs onto it. The other end of the molecule loves water and grabs onto it. With one end holding onto oily dirt, and the other holding onto water, soap acts as a link between the two, making it possible for water to wash the dirt away.

Materials *(for each group)*

plastic tarp (an old shower curtain works well) • wash tubs • water • mild laundry soap • 5 or more white cloth squares torn from an old sheet or towel, each stained with something (for example, ketchup, soil, molasses, tempera paint, mustard)
(for the class) clothesline (strung across the classroom) and clothespins • "WATER ONLY" and "SOAP AND WATER" labels

What to Do

1 Spread plastic tarps on the floor. Fill tubs with warm water and place on the tarps. Add soap to some tubs, while leaving others with just water.

2 Ask: Does washing with soap and water really clean better than just water alone? Tell students that they are going to find out. Agree on a washing technique and explain that everyone will wash their cloths the same way. However, some will be washing with just water, while others will use soap and water.

3 Divide the class into groups and give each group a stained cloth and a scrap of paper for labeling the stain. Using whatever technique was agreed on, have students wash the cloths.

4 Let students hang the cloths (with the labels) on the clothesline in the correct "WATER ONLY" or "SOAP AND WATER" sections.

5 When the cloths are dry, ask: Were any stains washed away with just water? Which look cleaner—those washed with water, or those with soap and water? Does soap help water clean better?

Critical Thinking Questions

Remind students how soap made a water drop flatten out. (See "Break Down," page 26.) Ask: What might soap do to water so that it cleans better? (Changes it somehow so that the water can wash away the dirt.)

What other factors might affect how clean the cloths got? (water temperature, kind of soap, amount of scrubbing)

Water Protection

This poster-making activity helps children appreciate why we need to respect and take care of water, a limited and valuable resource.

Materials

pictures and news articles about water pollution and threatened wetlands • large white paper • crayons or paints

What to Do

1 Discuss what can happen to water supplies and environments when people are careless. Use pictures and news articles as discussion aids.

2 Have children think of ways to conserve and protect different sources of water. Review: How can we use less water? Why is it important to be careful not to waste water? What can we do to help keep water clean?

3 Have students write slogans about protecting and using water wisely. Then choose a slogan for a poster to make on drawing paper.

4 Using paints or crayons, have children illustrate their slogans with pictures. Display these posters in the room or hallway.

Literature Connection

In *Chubbo's Pool*, by Betsy Lewin, and *It's Mine!*, by Leo Lionni, children learn about limited resources and how selfish and unselfish animals react. Both books are good references about our limited water resources.

Extension

FABRIC ART Help students make T-shirts or banners advertising water conservation. Use solid-colored T-shirts (these can be students' used shirts), or a sheet cut into squares, and the slogans from the previous activity. Children can decorate these with fabric paints or markers, plus large iron-on patches.

Science Background

Water covers more than 70 percent of the Earth's surface. Yet only 1 percent is fit for consumption. (Ninety-seven percent is salt water and the other 2 percent is fresh water trapped in glacier ice.) Over half of that is inaccessible, far beneath the Earth's surface.

CHAPTER 8

Wrap-Up

End your unit on water with a Water Works Celebration to emphasize for children the importance of learning. This is also the time to help students evaluate what they've learned.

Water Works Celebration

Students will enjoy sharing what they have learned with another class or with parents. Here are some ideas for planning a festive event to culminate your water unit.

Invitations

To prepare for the celebration, children will enjoy making invitations on paper cut in the shape of water drops. Decorate these with colored drops, which children make by dripping water colored with food coloring from different heights. After the drops are dry, students write their invitational message.

Displays

Plan with students how to set up your classroom to show off their completed projects. Display your best initial warm-up activities from Chapter One, such as the Opening Prior Knowledge Questions, the KWL wall chart, or the Learning Web. Make a display label that explains how you used these.

Display students' favorite creations: their Science Journals, water habitat models (page 52), water poem mobiles (page 56), finished boats (page 57), experiment charts, artwork, and writing projects. Have children write brief explanations of what they learned from each and use these as part of your evaluation process as well as for the display.

Let children demonstrate their awareness of the importance of water and water conservation by wearing their T-shirts or displaying banners from page 59, or sharing slogans and poetry.

Wet the Appetite

Plan some water-based treats to make and serve. Children might want to make a gelatin dessert, frozen water treats made from orange juice or lemonade, or perhaps serve watermelon or other juicy fruits, and water, of course!

Entertainment

Set up student-directed stations where guests get a chance to try some of the water investigations. (See "Penny Drops" on page 24, for example, or "I'm Melting!" on page 35.) Ask students to be responsible for choosing an experiment, helping with the set-up, and explaining what to do at each station.

Other entertainment could include a production of the play Going in Cycles (pages 41–42), or playing a game of Water Charades (page 12).

Evaluation

You'll find considerable value in having students do some of the evaluation process themselves. As they revisit what they have learned through their artwork and Journal writing, have them highlight new concepts. Ask: How and where do these fit on our KWL chart? Fill in the chart as needed to help them feel proud of their progress and new understanding.

Similarly, return to the Prior Knowledge Questions and Learning Web presented in Chapter One. Ask: What have we learned that helps us answer these questions? What do we still need to find out? Come up with a plan for further investigations.

Encourage children to continue to make water the focus of their observations and discoveries, inviting them to share their ongoing experiences. Give them copies of journal page 62 to complete and add to their Science Journals, setting the stage for more open-ended opportunities.

Name _____

What I Learned About Water

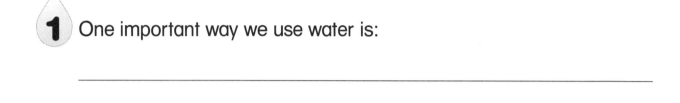 **1** One important way we use water is:

_____

_____

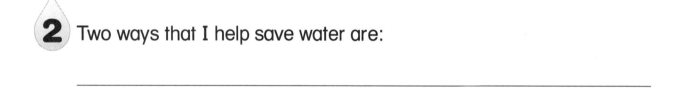 **2** Two ways that I help save water are:

_____

_____

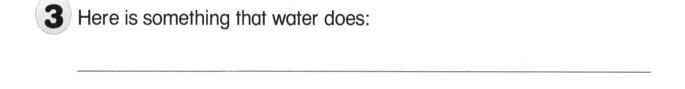 **3** Here is something that water does:

_____

_____

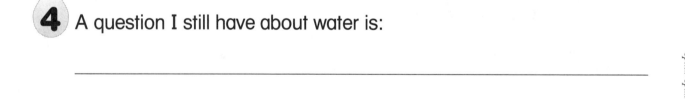 **4** A question I still have about water is:

_____

_____

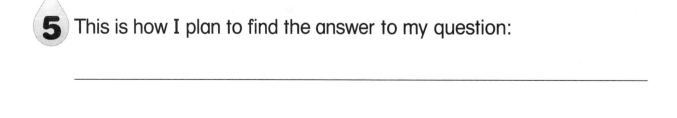 **5** This is how I plan to find the answer to my question:

_____

_____

Splish-Splash Science Scholastic Professional Books

Classroom Resources

Literature

Chubbo's Pool by Betsy Lewin; Clarion Books, 1996

The Cloud Book by Tomie dePaola; Holiday House, 1975

Cloud Nine by Norma Silver; Clarion Books, 1995

Ducklings and Pollywogs by Anne Rockwell; Macmillan, 1994

* *Emily's Snowball: The World's Biggest* by Elizabeth Keown; Macmillan, 1992

The House at Pooh Corner by A.A. Milne; E.P. Dutton, 1928

It's Mine by Leo Lionni; Alfred A. Knopf, 1996

Jack's Fantastic Voyage by Michael Foreman; Harcourt Brace Jovanovich, 1992

Little Beaver and the Echo by Amy MacDonald; G.P. Putnam's Sons, 1990

The Mud Flat Olympics by James Stevenson; Greenwillow Books, 1994

Muskrat Will Be Swimming by Cheryl Savageau; Northland Publishing, 1996

The Piggy in the Puddle by Charlotte Pomerantz; Macmillan, 1974

Puddles by Jonathan London; Viking, 1997

The Puddle Pail by Elisa Kleven; Dutton, 1997

The Rain by Michael Laser; Simon & Schuster, 1997

*Rain by Peter Spier; Doubleday, 1982

The Rainbow Fish by Marcus Pfister; North-South Books, 1992

Sail Away by Donald Crews; Greenwillow Books, 1995

Sand in My Shoes by Wendy Kesselman; Hyperion Books, 1995

*Sea Gifts by George Shannon; David Godine Publisher, 1989

Three Days on a River in a Red Canoe by Vera B. Williams; Mulberry Books, 1981

Very Last First Time by Jan Andrews; Macmillan, 1986

Wet World by Norma Simon; Candlewick Press, 1995

Poetry

In the Swim: Poems & Paintings by Douglas Florian; Harcourt Brace, 1997

Listen to the Rain by Bill Martin, Jr., and John Archambault; Henry Holt, 1988

Once Upon Ice and Other Frozen Poems selected by Jane Yolen; Boyds Mills, 1997

Rain Song by Lezlie Evans and Cynthia Jabar; Houghton Mifflin, 1995

Rainsong/Snowsong by Philemon Sturges and Shari Halpern; North-South Books, 1995

Nonfiction

At the Frog Pond by Tilde Michels; Lippincott, 1989

Caring for Our Water by Carol Greene; Enslow Publishers, 1991

A Drop of Water: A Book of Science and Wonder by Walter Wick; Scholastic, 1997

Disappearing Wetlands by Helen J. Challand; Children's Press, 1992

Experiment with Water by Bryan Murphy; Lerner Publications, 1991

Follow the Water from Brook to Ocean by Arthur Dorros; HarperCollins, 1991

I Am Water by Jean Marzollo; Scholastic, 1996

Liquid to Gas & Back by J. M. Patten; Rourke Book Company, 1995

One Small Square: Pond (also *Seashore* and *Swamp*) by Donald M. Silver and Patricia J. Wynne; McGraw Hill, 1994

Pond and Brook by Michael Caduto; University Press of New England, 1990

Pond Life by Frank Greenaway; Dorling Kindersley, 1992

Squish! A Wetland Walk by Nancy Luenn; Atheneum, 1994

The Stream by Naomi Russell; Dutton, 1990

Turtles, Toads, and Frogs by George Fichter; Western Publishing, 1993

Water by Frank Asch; Gulliver Green, 1995

Water by Andrew Charman; Raintree Steck-Vaughn, 1994

Water by Graham Peacock; Thomson Learning, 1994

The Water Cycle by David Smith; Thomson Learning, 1993

Wetlands by Linda Stone; Rourke, 1989

Wow! The Wonders of Wetlands by Alan Kesselheim and Britt Slattery; Environmental Concern, Inc. and The Watercourse, 1995

What Do You See in a Cloud? by Allan Fowler; Children's Press, 1996

Where Do Puddles Go? by Fay Robinson; Children's Press, 1995

Software

Ducks Ahoy!; Joyce Hakansson Associates, 1984

A Field Trip into the Sea; Sunburst Communications, 1992

Fish Scales; DLM, 1985

Sammy's Science House; Edmark Corporation, 1994

Videos and Audiotapes

Circle of Water (National Geographic Society, product number G51723). This video lets viewers take an imaginary trip through the water cycle.

Wilderness Thunderstorm by NorthSounds (NorthWord Press, 1992). From the pitter-patter of a gentle rain to a rumbling thunderstorm, children will be enthralled by the sounds of rainy days on this audiotape.

* Out of print. Check your library for a circulating copy.